SOLO STANDING ON GUARD

Abhijit Naskar is the twenty-first century Neuroscientist whose contributions in Cognitive and Behavioral Neuroscience have helped the world tackle the issues of systemic racism, prejudice, hate, extremism, discrimination and biases more effectively. As an untiring advocate of mental health and universal acceptance, he became a beloved best-selling author all over the world with his very first book "The Art of Neuroscience in Everything". With his pioneering ventures into the Neuropsychology of beliefs and biases, he has hugely contributed in the eradication of religious and cultural differences in our world, for which he is popularly hailed as the humanitarian scientist, who takes the human civilization in the path of sweet general harmony.

Solo Standing On Guard

Life Before Law

ABHIJIT NASKAR

Solo Standing on Guard: Life Before Law

Copyright © 2021 Abhijit Naskar

This is a work of non-fiction

An Amazon Publishing Company, 1st Edition, 2021

Printed in the United States of America

ISBN: 9798744829230

Lives to Serve Before I Sleep
When Humans Unite: Making A World Without Borders
All For Acceptance
Monk Meets World
Mission Reality
Citizens of Peace: Beyond The Savagery of Sovereignty
Operation Justice: To Make A Society That Needs No Law
See No Gender
The Gospel of Technology
Every Generation Needs Caretakers: The Gospel of
Patriotism
Aşkanjali: The Sufi Sermon
Mad About Humans: World Maker's Almanac
Revolution Indomable
When Call The People: My World My Responsibility
No Foreigner Only Family
Hurricane Humans: Give me accountability, I'll give you
peace
Ain't Enough to Look Human
Servitude is Sanctitude
Time To End Democracy: The Meritocratic Manifesto
I Vicdansaadet Speaking: No Rest Till The World is Lifted
Boldly Comes Justice: Sentient not Silent
Good Scientist: When Science and Service Combine
Sleepless for Society
Neden Türk: The Gospel of Secularism
Martyr Meets World: To Solve The Hard Problem of
Inhumanity
The Shape of A Human: Our America Their America
When Veins Ignite: Either Integration or Degradation
Heart Force One: Need No Gun to Defend Society

DEDICATION

To the activists who don't call themselves activist.

CONTENTS

1. Human and Society are One

You can take the humanitarian out of the society, but you can't take society out of the humanitarian, for society is the lifeblood of the humanitarian - concern for society runs through every molecule of the humanitarian. In fact, the humanitarian and the society are not separate, but one. Or to put it simply, the human and the society are not separate, but one.

The very title human is a revolution in itself - it's a revolution of love against the atrocities of hate. There are words I don't want to use, such as humanitarian, martyr and so on, but I am compelled to use them - you know why, because the society is incapable of grasping the gravitas of the word human. Once you witness the universe of warmth and accountability the title human contains within, all other words of glory will fade away.

One who realizes the gravitas of the title human, needs no bible to tell right from wrong. They don't need to go to church either, for their very footsteps trigger a cascade of divinity. What is divinity, if not an everyday sense of kindness! What is humanity, if not an everyday sense of kindness!

One who realizes the gravitas of the title human, needs no constitution to tell right from wrong. They don't need congress to bring reform in the society, for their very footsteps embody all the reform that is needed. You know what reform is - reform is potential realized - reform is accountability in action. Therefore, absence of reform is absence of accountability - and absence of accountability is absence of humanity.

2.   MCA: Middle Class Activist
(The Sonnet)

MCA: Middle Class Activist
(The Sonnet)

I don't know the meaning of socialism,
But progress without society is insanity.
I don't know the meaning of capitalism,
But catering to luxury produces disparity.
I don't know the meaning of woke,
But no life is complete without community.
I don't know the meaning of philosophy,
But intellect is useless without amity.
I don't own many fancy gadgets,
Affording essentials I stand without greed.
I'll probably never set foot on MARS,
On earth I'll be serving the abandoned in need.
High and mighty tech won't make this world better,
Till we place humanity at our highest altar.

3. When Inclusion is not Inclusion

A human without accountability is not a human to begin with. There is nothing more beautiful than the sight of an accountable human being - you know why - because if you want to see reckless liberty, you can find it plenty in the jungle.

In some intellectual circles these humans of accountability are called humanitarians - that's because, as I said earlier, the term human is too bland, and people are drawn to ideologies and concepts that have some pomposity attached to them. Simplicity has no value and complexity is everything, therefore, insecurity has become the norm and serenity mere phantom.

I am a human being - this very statement ought to say everything worth knowing about a human, rest should be mere detail - yet, in the world we live in, the statement - I am a human - means absolutely nothing - on top of that, when you introduce yourself with a so-called practical alternative, people automatically come up with your worth in their head, driven by their predominant biases.

And even if you do not introduce yourself, people assume your worth based on your outlook, just like they assume your worth based on the color of your skin. For example, in a so-called civilized world, a person with white skin is worth more than a person of color – thus they receive privileges in every walk of society, whereas the person of color faces doubt and suspicion every step of the way.

The mind makes stereotypes, because the mind wants to survive. Conquer those stereotypes and you'll start to live, not as animal but as human. Beyond stereotypes there is life - a life where realization and action are valued more than labels and appearance. And the beginning of that life my friend is the birth of a human being.

When compassion is no longer compassion, but simply love, that's the awakening of the human being. When kindness is no longer kindness, but simply existence, that's the awakening of the human being. When inclusion is no longer inclusion, but simply being, that's the awakening of the human being.

4. Sonnet of Care

Sonnet of Care

This is what care looks like,
Pure and chaste loving without reward.
This is what conscience looks like,
Strong and just reasoning with warmth.
This is what nobility looks like,
Humble and kind correcting one's error.
This is what courage looks like,
Firm and unbending walking across fear.
This is what sentience looks like,
Awake and upright marching with resolve.
This is what character looks like,
Messy and flawed but not afraid to evolve.
Each human is a reflection of all humanity.
Individual action determines collective destiny.

5. You Are Your Authority

There is no need for more ideologies - there is no need for more philosophies - there is no need for more sects. - what's needed is the desire to step beyond all sectarianism. I was not born to raise yet another sect, the world is infested with plenty sects already. I was born to raise Gods to step across those sects and make the whole world their family. When all separations vanish and you see the whole world as family, that's the real beginning of your human life.

Help others not because you feel bad for them, but because you see yourself in them. This is the only secret to life - serve others as your own reflection. This is the secret to civilization - a civilization where the civilized beings need no external intervention of authority to determine right from wrong.

A civilized human recognizes values, not authority, for when there is accountability, there is no need for authority. So long as you need law to tell you what is right, what is wrong, don't tell anyone you are human. So long as you need the church to tell you what is right, what is wrong, don't tell anyone you are human.

Human mind is the authority of human life, nothing else - nothing is higher than the mind, nothing is more capable than the mind. But mark you, here we are not talking about matters of expertise, rather we are talking about matters of everyday ordinary living - the matters of right and wrong, the matters of good and evil, the matters of humanity and inhumanity, the matters of sanity and insanity, the matters of civilization and savagery. In all these matters, you are to be your own light, you are to be your own guide, you are to be your own sight.

6. Constitutional Fundamentalism

No constitution is going to tell you what is human, what is not. They may try, but that's all. The efforts of the constitution to determine human behavior is not to be confused with the measure of human behavior. Let me elaborate.

Human rights and constitutional rights are not the same thing. Constitutional rights are human attempt to preserve human rights through legislative means. Therefore, constitutional rights must keep evolving to actually preserve human rights.

What might have seemed to be a constitutional right two hundred years ago may not apply in today's society and what may seem to be a constitutional right today may not apply to the society of the future. Therefore, no constitutional right is to be taken as gospel, they must be scrutinized by each new generation and if found incompatible with the new society, must be either amended or discarded altogether.

If you treat the constitution the same way fundamentalists treat the bible, you are going to have a very sick society on your hands. This is what I call constitutional fundamentalism, which is as dangerous as religious fundamentalism.

The constitutional right of today may be a violation of human rights tomorrow, hence, no constitution, and in fact, no text is to be taken as gospel. For example, bearing firearm may have been a constitutional right of every citizen back in the days when life across America was practically a western movie, but now that we have established law and order, that right is no longer valid.

In the same way, what is considered blasphemy today may turn into a constitutional right tomorrow. For example, same-sex marriage remained excluded from our constitutional right to life, liberty and pursuit of happiness till 2015. Today it is legal not only in our United States, but more and more countries are accepting it as basic human right.

So you see, human rights itself is subject to human scrutiny. Constitution comes later, first the humans must have a firm grasp of human rights - we must have a firm grasp of our basic humanity – and more importantly, we must have the genuine desire for growth.

We may consider something wrong due to our lack of knowledge, but in the face of overwhelming evidence only an animal refuses to change their outlook and persists with their delusions. This may be acceptable from the fragile, elderly population, but the young and energetic must rise above such outdated behavior.

7. Sonnet of Nation Building

Sonnet of Nation Building

Nation means not land,
Nation means not border.
Nation means sentience and sanity,
Nation means willing to treat disorder.
Nation means not habit,
Nation means not tradition.
Nation means reason and acceptance,
Nation means conscious amalgamation.
Nations mean not law,
Nations mean not policy.
Nation means a genuine goodness,
Nation means an accountable citizenry.
In the name of nation do not act tribal.
Nation without narrowness is a land universal.

8. Being Law-Abiding is not Civilized

Everything that lives must evolve. Therefore, everything that society lives by must evolve as well, be it the constitution, be it the bible, be it law, or in fact, be it any other moving part on the fabric of society. Rigid obedience to anything is but a denial of life. So how can you exist as a living being, when you deny life itself?

Life first then everything else. Law is there to preserve and protect life, not to harm it. It must always be, life before law, people before policy. People are not supposed to be at the mercy of law, law is supposed to be at the mercy of people. In a civilized society, it's the people that law is supposed to serve, yet it's the people who end up serving the law - and this spineless obedience is further reinforced by the title "law-abiding citizen".

In short, if you are law-abiding, you are considered righteous, while the officers and the makers may be committing the most unrighteous acts in history. To put it simply, lawkeepers and lawmakers are not the authority of society - they are mere public servant. The term "public servant" may seem simple enough, yet it holds the entire definition of a civilized society within its syllables.

The term "public servant" entails that no matter how authoritative and high almighty such an individual acts in society, the harness to their power is always in the hands of the people - or to put it in lay terms, it's the people who are the authority of the officers as well as the makers of law, not the other way around. So, when a police officer or a politician goes bonkers, go out there and stand, until they are fired.

What this entails is that, as long as law defends the people against inhumanity, it may be entitled to the approval of the people, but the moment it turns against people, whether willingly or driven by subconscious biases, then it is the duty of the people to stand up with unarmed, nonviolent determination and fire such lawkeepers and lawmakers.

Politicians and police are not the makers and keepers of law, the people are. Unless the people live a life of accountability, there'll be no order in society, but only an illusion of order. Real order is born of accountability - the real one, not the fake one - the accountability that doesn't let you sit still when you someone in distress- the accountability that makes you restless when you see injustice happening in front of your eyes.

Only with such everyday, ordinary, genuine accountability can we instill real lasting order in society.

9. Beyond The Phantom of Hope

It is not about hope, it is not about expectations and anticipation - it's this simple, either you act or you don't, there's no hoping. I am not asking you to be hopeless or hopeful, I am asking you to look at reality as it is, beyond hope - a reality that is born of cruelty but with the potential for amity - a reality that demands tangible human intervention - the mere phantom of hope won't do.

You see, those who do, don't have time for hopes and prayers - they are too busy causing the change to even think about hoping or praying for change. Let others hope and pray all they want, but as for you, the being of conscience and character, throw away all hopes and prayers and leap into action. Remember, where there is accountability, there is action, where there is indifference, there is prayer. Be the action my friend. Be the miracle that everybody hopes for.

There is no greater miracle in the world, than a human devoted to a cause - a cause that doesn't only elevate the self, but also the society. A cause that only benefits you and does nothing for the people around is no cause, but a mere waste of life.

Miracle is not turning wine into water, real miracle is to share your last glass of water with someone thirsty. Such is the character of a leader. A leader never says I am here to lead, a leader says, I am here to serve. And indeed, such is the character of a human being – a character immersed in service, all else is mere mockery of human life.

You must be prepared to lay down your life for the betterment of the people, only then can there be real civilization in this world - only then can there be real humanity in this world. Civilization starts with selflessness, for the entire animal kingdom is predicated on selfishness.

10. Be The Future

Contrary to popular belief, selflessness doesn't mean giving up all your material possessions - selflessness means having an everyday, ordinary and uncorrupted concern for others. Thus, possessions have no bearing here - you could be a rich entrepreneur and yet live a life of selflessness by simply reaching out to those in distress. When you reach out to the helpless with a gesture of kindness in your daily walks of life, that is called selflessness - and not just that - that is the very definition of righteous human behavior.

Lay yourself down for others and even the mountains will lay themselves down at your feet to make way for you. Books, intellect, facts - all these are mere dust in front of love. Bring that love out for society - a love that defies all assumptions, a love that defies all habits, a love that defies all norms - a love that is pure and chaste and needs no praise.

In your love the world will find its way - in your strength the world will find its courage - in your light the world will witness its future. We cannot actually build the future, we have to be the future. Be a living manifestation of the future my friend - a future where selflessness is the norm and selfishness is disease, a future where warmth is the way and arrogance is obsolete, a future where assimilation is sanity and bigotry is a clinical condition.

We have been raising walls through millennia, it's time we be the ladder. Be the ladder my friend. Always say, I don't care for meditation, I don't care for illumination, I only care for collective ascension - not personal mark you, but collective. What is personal must become collective, what is collective must become personal.

11. Shades of Brown
(The Sonnet)

Shades of Brown
(The Sonnet)

There is no white skin,
There is no black skin.
All of us are shades of brown,
If we can reason without stereotyping.
Climate makes the difference in color,
But not in character of the individual.
Human character knows no geography,
For a being of character is human above all.
The idea of race is a myth most foul,
Born of ignorance and narrowness.
Now we live in a different time,
That requires abolition of divisiveness.
Discard those traditions and live as sapient.
Let's build a world where color ain't relevant.

12. Relics of Civilized Society

Dare and do not despair. Dare to love, dare to reason, dare to live, without caution. There are mainly two kinds of people in the world, those who forget to live due to caution, and those who forget to live due to sheer recklessness - then there are those few handful of bravehearts who conquer all caution and live with utmost regard for and accountability of human life - these are the lionhearted soldiers of civilization who can revolutionize this world and turn it from a good-looking animal kingdom into a civilized and conscientious human society - a society that lives beyond duality - a society that lives without the desire for codification of righteousness - a society that lives beyond argumentations of definitions.

I'll say it plainly - if you can identify yourself without resorting to any societal terminologies, then and then only will the human in you have real civilized birth. Otherwise, if you think four little alphabets, w-o-k-e, can define civilized human life, you are as dumb as those you consider un-woke. It is another way to codify righteousness, just like the church does with the term "born again". Be human my friend - beyond wokeness - beyond religiousness -

beyond intellectualism and all forms of binarism and sectarianism.

Sectarianism has no place upon the fabric of a civilized society. That's why I say, leave your crown, your constitution, your scripture outside when you enter my door. In an actual civilized society, crowns, constitutions and scriptures may exist only as relics of humankind's struggling past, and not as authorities of the present.

When I close my eyes, I can see the world of my dream clear as day - a world where there is no man, there is no woman, there is no queer, there is only love - a world where there is no white, there is no color, there is only love - a world where there is no believer, there is no non-believer, there is only love - a world where there is no leader, there is no follower, there is only love. This is the civilization that we must build - a civilization that has conquered its animal nature rather being conquered by it - a civilization that is human at heart, human at thought, and human in action.

13. Books Over Bombs
(The Sonnet)

Books Over Bombs
(The Sonnet)

Bombs kill terrorists,
Books kill terrorism.
Missiles kill extremists,
Mindfulness kills extremism.
Guns kill supremacists,
Goodness kills supremacy.
Law restrains cruel people,
Love reforms cruelty.
Sarin cripples the malicious,
Service cures malice.
C4 impairs the prejudiced,
Curiosity treats prejudice.
Violence can be revolution no more.
For all degradation kindness is the cure.

14. Love Needs No Etiquette

Be the love and there will be love. One ounce of love is more powerful than a hundred pounds of intellect. But mark you, that love must be genuine, without compulsion, without hope, without expectation - that love is to be the very expression of your existence, nothing short of it would do.

The being of love doesn't need any etiquette to be accepted in society, because the being of love is not a part of society, they are the highest manifestation of a civilized society - whatever is civilized is born from them. It's the shallow creatures that try to make up for their shallowness with etiquette.

The civilized human stands firm on their conviction and says, I don't obey no etiquette, I don't obey no norm - whatever is civilized is born of me, whatever is human is born of me. Remember, the mountain doesn't bow to no one in obedience. If the mountain bows, it is in humility. Be the mountain and stand true on your core conviction with your last ounce of life.

If you are true to your core, loving, caring and indivisible, you have no need for pretenses, such as etiquettes and law, it's only when you are empty inside, that you need etiquettes and law. And behold, we have a society full of etiquettes and law, but no substance in them to speak of.

When you have love, you are accountable, and when you are accountable, you become the living source of all things civilized, but when there is no love, there is no accountability, and where there is no accountability, even a thousand constitutions and bibles fall short to make a civilized human out of you.

15. No Compromise
(The Sonnet)

No Compromise
(The Sonnet)

Only cowards make compromise,
When it comes to affairs of humanity.
Beings of conscience and character,
Prefer revolution over indignity.
Only bugs bow before oppression,
Driven by insecurity and indifference.
Creatures called the homo sapiens,
Choose annihilation before compliance.
Only wild animals of the cruel jungle,
Accept self-preservation as the norm.
For advanced organism such as humans,
Inclusion is life in joy and in storm.
Those with backbone stand up for humanity.
Unarmed and unbending we'll conquer inhumanity.

16. Thou Art Civilization

The very mission of my life is to set in motion an uprising of unbending, civilized lionhearts who would stand firm on their conviction and say, "I'll rescue humanity from the clutches of prejudice, bias and disparity, even if it means giving up my serenity." Remember, it is far better to break for your conviction than to bend for nothing.

We are to be the originators of a real civilized society and the power to do that is already vested in us. What this world needs is a new kind of patriotism - patriotism not for a nation or religion or ideology - but for the whole of humankind. The whole world must become family, once it is, right action flows on its own, without argumentation, without duality. In fact, call yourself human the day you see everyone as family, not before that.

Say to yourself, I am the sun, no one can give me anything, but I have plenty to give everyone. Stand tall as a rock - as a pillar of strength - indestructible, incorruptible, insurmountable - and at the very sight of you half the world will turn civilized. Bring all your light out into the world. The task will not be finished till all humans become the personification of civilization.

Remember, it is the humans that make civilization, not the other way around. Figure it out, thou art civilization. There is nothing else - there is nothing in the Capitol, there is nothing in the Vatican. If you don't find civilization inside you, you won't find it anywhere.

In every walk of life, nature will force you to be selfish. If you can conquer that force and be unselfish instead, you'll conquer the world. Trash your meditation, trash your rituals, trash your argumentation, and give yourself to the making of a civilized world - the mission for which I burnt myself to ashes.

17. The Temper Sonnet

The Temper Sonnet

Where you need to be calm,
You burst out in rage.
Where you need to be on fire,
You walk in silence and not engage.
Where you need to listen,
You scream like a loudspeaker.
Where you need to speak out,
Somehow your words disappear.
Where it requires to be humble,
Pride takes over your humility.
Where your blood needs to boil,
Your veins seem to run empty.
The right use of temper is an act of revolution.
Put it to good use and you'll nourish civilization.

18. When Conviction and Humility Combine

The civilized human says, "I am not a man or woman, separated from society, I am the whole society - a society that is inclusive not exclusive, a society that is accepting not segregating, a society that is expanding not narrowing." When every nation has ten such civilized beings with nerves of thunder and hearts of honey, a thousand years of progress will take place in a year.

The making of that world is no work of spineless vegetables, it requires tremendous determination. Cowards have no role here, which means, their being and not being are the same. What is required is an absolute defiance of indifference. Defy your indifference and inhumanity will lose half its strength. Defy indifference, apply reason and rise up with warmth. You are my soldier of ascension, you are my warrior of inclusion - never forget that. The whole world will fall short for my army of unarmed humanitarians.

Strength is the servant of conviction. If your conviction is awake, then no weakness can overpower you. If your conviction is awake, then your mind will manufacture strength at your command. So cater not to weakness, embrace it and work through it in the course of your conviction, and before long it'll disappear into thin air.

But mark you, it is crucial that you do not confuse conviction with arrogance. Humility is what needed, not arrogance. When conviction and humility combine, something magical happens to the world - it turns from a savage, self-centric, prejudiced kingdom of animals to a civilized, community-centric, self-regulated and evolving society of humans - humans with gentleness, humans with simplicity, humans with humor, without the least bit of egotistical inhumanity, be it intellectual, nationalistic or any other.

19. The Commitment Sonnet

The Commitment Sonnet

Once you commit to something,
Better give up life than the commitment.
Once you make a promise,
Better stop breathing than break it.
Once you realize your purpose,
Better be destroyed than forget it.
Once you stand on your conviction,
Better be broken to pieces than lose it.
Submit, submit, o braveheart,
Submit to something bigger than the self.
Wipe out the self if necessary,
Give all to your goal asking no help.
Life has no meaning except self-preservation.
Your destiny is determined by your action.

20. Till Kindness Becomes First Nature

Never entertain arrogance, be it in yourself or in others. Wherever you see arrogance, either overwhelm it with your absolute and utter simplicity or walk away. You see, you'll learn more about life from the stand-up of a responsible comedian than from the literature of an egotistical intellectual. Arrogance and life cannot go hand in hand - human life that is. Either you are arrogant, or you are an alive human, you cannot be both.

It is a slippery slope from arrogance to violence. Hence, pride, arrogance, egotism - all these must be thrown away at once. They are all manifestations of the instinctual drive for self-preservation, and as such, they serve well in the animal kingdom, but they have no place in a civilized society. That is why, even our acts of revolution must take place without the influence of these primitive tendencies, for sooner or later they all lead to violence.

But here is the question. Why isn't it justified to resort to violence in the course of justice? It's because if you resort to violence for your conviction of humanity, then nothing stops the inhumans to resort to violence for their conviction. Hence nothing changes. We must change the very notion that it is okay to resort to violence if we want to change the society. While it may have been okay in the past, it is not okay any more, because it is not civilized. Therefore what's needed is a desire for reform founded entirely on the premise of peace.

The civilized human must set an example of civilized behavior. And when enough civilized humans thus set an example of civilized behavior in their everyday life, only then the archaic paradigm of cruelty will be washed away by the new, life-giving torrents of gentleness.

Let me put it another way, until our first nature turns from cruelty to kindness, there'll be no progress, no matter how much advancement we make in terms of technology. An ape driving a Tesla is still an ape. We must advance internally first. Once we achieve that all things external will become easy. Let the external advancements continue if they must, but make sure the primary attention is on internal advancement.

21. Internal Advancement First

All external advancements are to serve the humans, not the other way around. And without internal advancement, the human society will continue to end up as mere slave to external, material advancements.

External advancements don't just mean technological and scientific advancement, they also include advancement in societal constructs, such as the constitution, law enforcement, government and so on. And when you focus solely on societal constructs, rather than on the education and nourishment of the individual mind, you have a society that looks civilized on the outside, yet functions no different from a tribe of cannibals.

As a result, you have law enforcement officials corrupt to the bones with prejudice, you have government involved purely in partisan politics, you have intellectuals involved in never-ending philosophical argumentation and so on.

Let me elaborate with a few examples. Let's take politics first. There is not one but two politics. One is simply politics, which involves the welfare of the people, and the other is partisan politics, which involves the welfare of one party over that of other parties as well as the welfare of the people. This latter one is what commonly referred to in society as politics – and indeed this is the politics what we primarily have in nations across the world. Yet it is the politics involved in human welfare that can improve human condition in society, which can only happen if the individuals involved pay attention to the purpose and not the means - that is, they are to pay attention to the benefit of the people, and not the glorification of particular political ideologies.

Likewise, no policy can turn animal officers of the law into human officers of the law, for police reform starts with the acknowledgement of police bias. So to the keepers of law I say, dear officers of the law, if you find it difficult to maintain order without being a badge-bearing barbarian, seek professional help, for you are ill, terribly ill, and the cure for your illness is education.

Education, education, education - education of not the person, but the psyche - that's how we'll reform this society - or to be blatant - that's how we'll turn an animal kingdom into a human society. There is no two way about it - either we recognize our biases and work incessantly to overwhelm them with civilized thought, emotions and behavior, or after a short flight of shallow, disparity-driven advancement, fall of the lifeform called sapiens is ensured.

Order can't be forced. If it is forced, it's not real order. Let me elaborate with an example. Let's take the United Kingdom. There is no such thing as her majesty's government. You can either have his or her majesty or you can have government. You cannot have both. No government is civilized till it abolishes all allegiance to monarchy. And a government that is not civilized, is not much of a government. Likewise, you can either be a subject or a citizen, you cannot be both, for the title citizen involves individual thought, whereas the title subject involves absolute thoughtless loyalty to an archaic paradigm that is suitable only for jungle creatures.

Any system that facilitates allegiance to pedigree or popularity is a most disgusting stain upon the honor of a civilized society. So, to the people who are still living under the delusion of royal superiority, I say, grow up. But again, apparently the only way we can make people do something honorable right away is by banning the unrighteous bits from society. So in this case, the only way to end monarchy is to ban monarchy altogether. But as I said, you may think that you are making civilized beings out of people by banning uncivilized behavior, all you are really doing is forcing people to suppress their uncivilized tenets.

Trying to make the society walk the line with law is like trying to control children by frightening them of the boogieman. Unless these children foster a genuine sense of responsibility and righteousness towards society out of their own free will, no one can make civilized beings out of them. Until then, all you'll have is an illusion of civilization, not actual, tangible and lasting civilization. Therefore, the way out is not force but education. Only education will make way for the birth of real, heartfelt order - an order founded on love and accountability, rather than fear and insecurity.

24. Laws Don't Make Civilization

Till the world is made Aşkistan, that is, land of love, by individual initiative, all policy, diplomacy and assemblies are bound to fail. Some intellectuals here may most boastfully argue, aren't policy, diplomacy and assemblies the way to make the world a land of love! To which I say again, so long as you attempt to force reform onto the world by shallow external constructs, you are bound to fail.

So I repeat, the only way to reform the world is by reforming the psyche, and the only way to reform the psyche is through education - not education as in literacy or higher learning, but education as in a whole rejuvenation of the mind in the direction of reason, courage and assimilation.

Laws don't make a civilized society, only accountability does. Remove the laws and you'll see the real, uncivilized face of society, which means that the only thing that keeps people from being savages is the fear of law. So they pretend to be civilized. And pretending to be civilized and being actually civilized are not the same.

Any order that is achieved through fear of punishment is not real order, but only an illusion of order. Hence, this is not real civilization. It is a fake civilization. And fake civilizations don't last long, no matter how pompous and flashy they look on the outside.

Remove the law and see who continue to behave civilized - those are the real civilized humans, rest are mere animals in human's clothing. Without individual accountability, there is never going to be a civilized society in this world - an accountability that sees all society as family - an accountability in which the ascension of the individual is in the ascension of the collective.

Without the sense of collective ascension no advancement can ensure progress of the humankind, it'll only ensure the material elevation of the privileged class. And such sectarian elevation is not elevation but the worst kind of degradation there is.

25. Either Aşkistan or Junglistan
(A Sonnet)

Either Aşkistan or Junglistan
(A Sonnet)

Ours is either aşkistan,
Land of love founded on amity,
Or it is an archaic junglistan,
Run by contagious self-centricity.
What is civilized is also unselfish,
For selfishness makes the animal,
Across the self there is humanity,
What is unselfish is also accountable.
Technology may bring comfort,
But it doesn't ensure ascension,
When comfort belongs to the privileged,
Such progress is mere descension.
Over 3 billion years have gone in selfishness,
It's time to unself our soul and rise as sapiens.

26. What is Civilized is Unselfish

Selfishness is incompatible with the society of a civilized lifeform. Unself your soul and the world will be yours. A civilized lifeform is an unselfish lifeform A civilized lifeform is a nonsectarian lifeform. Sectarianism of any kind is indicative of selfishness, and a selfish lifeform is an uncivilized lifeform.

An unselfish human is the only human, rest are lesser replicas. And here is the intriguing part. An unselfish person is also a prideless person, an unselfish person is also a nonsectarian person, an unselfish person is also a humble person, and above all, an unselfish person is a civilized person. One of the three fundamental pillars of civilization is unselfishness, and the other two being reason and courage. A civilized society is an unselfish society, along with being ever-learning and courageous.

However, these are not really three separate ingredients, rather they are manifestations of each other. When you are unselfish, you care for others as family, and when your family is in danger courage appears on its own, so does the desire to learn for the benefit of those you care about. So in short, when you are unselfish, you are the maker of civilization, when selfish, you are the breaker.

Oneness blossoms in unselfishness, inclusion blossoms in unselfishness, ascension blossoms in unselfishness. And another name for unselfishness is civilization - another name for unselfishness is humanity - another name for unselfishness is love.

But I am not talking about theoretical love or romanticized love, I am talking about a love most chaste, a love that gives all and wants nothing back, a love that lives to love. If you can become such love, then only will you begin to discover the potential of human life. Until then you'll remain a slave to your self-serving instincts that still obey the one command of mother nature, kill or be killed.

I say again, unself your soul and apply that practical force of unselfishness in the treatment of inhumanities. The solution to a sick society is not rooted in policy, it is rooted in individual collectivity. What this means is, the laws and the policies of a democratic society can produce lasting result only if the everyday, ordinary individual feels one with their society - without sectarianism of any sort - be it racial sectarianism, be it religious sectarianism, be it gender or sexuality based sectarianism, be it intellectual sectarianism or any other. Be united with the world and the world will unite around you.

27. Reform is Not
A Legislative Issue

Politicians have to place all attention on policy, you know why - because if you remove the need for policy, you remove the need for politicians. And reform in policy may aid in the making of a reformed society, but it is not the cause of it. Unless the reform originates from the heart of the everyday, ordinary citizens, no policy can reform a society. You the individual, ordinary human must be the reform in your society, only then can there be real rejuvenation in your surroundings. Reform doesn't happen by force, it happens by example. That's why, reform is not a legislative issue, it is an individual accountability issue.

However, I am not opposing legislative attempts for reform, for there are many issues of society that can indeed be solved by legislative means, particularly the disparities born of a capitalistic abuse of resources. Therefore, the first and foremost function of a government, if it exists at all, is to eliminate all possible legal loopholes that sustain disparities in access to the essentials of life. To put it simply, in a civilized society, the government's foremost duty is to ensure equal distribution of essentials of life, and the citizens' foremost duty is to share the resources available to them with those without.

Government cannot make people civilized, but it can provide them the means to build their own destiny so that one day they no longer need to rely on any government. If we want to raise a civilized society, we must each work as per our capacities to end disparities. Inhumanity persists where there is disparity, eliminate the disparity and you'd automatically eliminate the need for inhumanity, at least those sustained by maldevelopment.

Hence I call for a treat-disparity movement as the first step of social reform. We cannot ensure justice and equality in a society whose very skeleton is made of self-centricity. We must replace it with community.

28. The Real Beginning of Life

There is not one but two types of self-centricity, one that persists due to the lack of resources, which torments many of the developing countries, and the other kind of self-centricity is the one founded on greed, which torments many of the developed countries. And the thrilling fact of the matter is, the solution to the former lies in the elimination of the latter.

What this means is that, if the advanced parts of the world could get rid of their greed in pursuit of their limitless productivity, and pays even a fraction of their attention on actually sharing their abundance of resources with those without, then we could easily do away with the savage paradigm that demands self-centricity in pursuit of survival.

However, the unfortunate reality is, when an entrepreneur becomes a billionaire by sucking all the resources from the world, nobody calls them a thief, yet when a homeless person steals a loaf of bread it is considered a heinous crime against humanity. If this is humanity, then I beg to report, you people are worse than animals. At least animals don't pretend to be civilized.

Let me put it another way. This is the gist of my life - I was born an animal, I burnt myself for humanity, I became human. And if you want to be the maker of a civilized world, then you must stand up and work towards raising the norm of sharing over greed. Criticizing the capitalist creeps does not end the disparities of the world. Be the gateway out of disparities yourself, however you can, and you'll see, change has been right around the corner.

I'll say it to you in simple words. Improve the living conditions and you'd automatically reduce crime rate. Improve the living conditions and you'd automatically reduce acts born of self-centricity driven by lack of resources. Here I do not expect much from the politicians, despite the fact that amidst the sea of self-obsessed and shallow political personalities, there are always some rare individuals truly working for the good of society, such as AOC.

True lasting reform in this direction can only come from the acts of the everyday, ordinary citizens who have the means to lift at least a small fraction of the society up on their shoulders. All you need to do, and that too not by compulsion, but due to accountability, is pull others up to a level where they are at the very least no longer destitute.

And you are not going to achieve it by giving in to the self-centric urges born of greed. You must distinguish what you need and what you don't, then use your excess resources to lift someone else up. I am not talking about charity. I am talking about helping someone get self-reliant, so that they don't need to rely on charity.

For example, if someone in your neighborhood is struggling to make ends meet, then why don't you gather some of your friends and raise funds to buy that person a food-truck or a hotdog stand. This way you are not only contributing at your individual capacity to the elimination of disparity, but more importantly you are helping a person live with dignity. And when someone regains their dignity because of you, that's the highest use of your human life.

Charity doesn't end disparity, for that, each citizen must become a government unto themselves - each citizen must become law unto themselves. In other words, each citizen must become a living constitution unto themselves, with the emphasis on living, which means ever-evolving and never-rigid. Be an example of growth in the world and the world will start to grow around you out of its disparities, biases and prejudices. Remember, great are those who build bridges with their heart's blood.

The fundamental requirement of a civilized life is the conquest of the world by individual accountability. To love is to be accountable, and to be accountable is to be human. There is only one way out of inhumanity - submission - yes you heard right, but not to any authority - the only way out of inhumanity is submission to love.

Give yourself fully to love, without any reservation whatsoever. Immerse yourself in the streams of love born of your own heart and the world around you will then bathe in that love of yours. In a civilized world, you either exist in love, or you don't exist at all. Life begins with the birth of love. Civilization begins with the birth of love.

BIBLIOGRAPHY

Archer M., (2000), Being Human: The Problem of Agency. Cambridge University Press.

Archer M., (2003), Structure, Agency and the Internal Conversation. Cambridge University Press.

Adolphs R (2003) Cognitive neuroscience of human social behaviour. Nature Rev Neurosci 4: 165–178.

Adolphs R, Tranel D, Damasio AR (2003) Dissociable neural systems for recognizing emotions. Brain Cogn 52: 61–69.

Afton, A. D. (1985). Forced copulation as a reproductive strategy of male lesser scaup: A field test of some predictions. - Behaviour 92, p. 146-167.

Allison T, Puce A, McCarthy G. (2000) Social perception from visual cues: role of the STS region. Trends Cogn Sci 4: 267–278.

Andresen, Jensine, and Robert Forman, eds. Cognitive Models and Spiritual Maps. Bowling Green, Ohio: Imprint Academic, 2000.

Ashbrook, James, and Carol Albright. The Humanizing Brain: Where Religion and Neuroscience Meet. Cleveland, OH: Pilgrim Press, 1997.

Azari, Nina, Janpeter Nickel, Gilbert Wunderlich, Michael Niedeggen, Harald Hefter, Lutz Tellmann, Hans Herzog, Petra Stoerig, Dieter Birnbacher, and Rudiger Seitz. "Neural Correlates of Religious Experience." European Journal of Neuroscience 13, no. 8 (2001)

Agar, N. (2004). Liberal eugenics: In defence of human enhancement. London: Blackwell Publishing.

Alteheld, N., Roessler, G., Vobig, M., & Walter, R. (2004). The retina implant new approach to a visual prosthesis. Biomedizinische Technik, 49(4), 99–103.

Antal, A., Nitsche, M. A., Kincses, T. Z., Kruse, W., Hoffmann, K. P., & Paulus, W. (2004a). Facilitation of visuo-motor learning by transcranial direct current stimulation of the motor and extrastriate visual areas in humans. European Journal of Neuroscience, 19(10), 2888–2892.

Bhat Z, Kumar, S, Bhat H (2015) In vitro meat production. Challenges and benefits over conventional meat production. J Sci Food Agric 14: 241–248

Bernstein R. J., (1967), John Dewey. New York: Washington Square Press.

Bernstein R.J., (1971), Praxis and Action: Contemporary Philosophies of Human Activity. Philadelphia: University of Pennsylvania Press.

Bernstein R.J., (1976), The Restructuring Social and Political Thought.

Bernstein R.J., (1983), Beyond Relativism and Objectivism: Science, Hermeneutics, and Praxis. Philadelphia: University of Pennsylvania Press.

Bernstein R.J., (1986), Philosophical Profiles. Philadelphia: University of Pennsylvania Press.

Bernstein R.J., (1991), New Constellation. Cambridge: MIT Press.

Barash, D. P. (1977). Sociobiology of rape in mallards (Anas platyrhynchos): Responses of the mated male. - Science 197, p. 788-789.

Berger, J. (1986). Wild horses of the great basin: Social competition and population size. - The University of Chicago Press, Chicago.

Birkhead, T. R., Johnson, S. D. & Nettleship, D. N. (1985). Extra-pair matings and mate guarding in the common murre Uria aalge. - Anim. Behav. 33, p. 608-619.

Beauregard, Mario, and Vincent Paquette. "Neural Correlates of a Mystical Experience in Carmelite Nuns." Neuroscience Letters 405, no. 3 (2006)

Benson, Herbert. Timeless Healing: The Power and Biology of Belief. New York: Scribner, 1996

Bose, Subhas Chandra. An Indian Pilgrim: An Unfinished Autobiography, Oxford University Press, 1997

Bose, Subhas Chandra. The Indian Struggle 1920-1942, Oxford University Press, 1997

Bogen, J.E.(1995a), 'On the neurophysiology of consciousness:

Part I. An overview', Consciousness and Cognition, 4.

Bogen, J.E. (1995b), 'On the neurophysiology of consciousness: Part II. Constraining the semantic problem', Consciousness and Cognition, 4.

Bremner, J. D., R. Soufer, et al. (2001). "Gender differences in cognitive and neural correlates of remembrance of emotional words." Psychopharmacol Bull 35 (3).

Brothers, L. (2002). The social brain: A project for integrating primate behavior and neurophysiology in a new domain. In J. T. Cacioppo et al. (Eds.), Foundations in neuroscience. Cambridge, MA: MIT Press.

Buss, D. D. (2003). Evolutionary Psychology: The New Science of Mind, 2nd ed. New York: Allyn & Bacon.

Buss, D. M. (1989). "Conflict between the sexes: Strategic interference and the evocation of anger and upset." J Pers Soc Psychol 56 (5).

Buss, D. M. (1995). "Psychological sex differences. Origins through sexual selection." Am Psychol 50 (3).

Buss, D. M. (2002). "Review: Human Mate Guarding." Neuro Endocrinol Lett 23 (Suppl 4).

Buss, D. M., and D. P. Schmitt (1993). "Sexual strategies theory: An evolutionary perspective on human mating." Psychol Rev 100 (2).

Blakemore SJ, Decety J (2001) From the perception of action to the understanding of intention. Nature Rev Neurosci 2: 561.

Bruce C, Desimone R, Gross CG (1981) Visual properties of neurons in a polysensory area in superior temporal sulcus of the macaque. J Neurophysiol 46: 369–384.

Buccino G, Vogt S, Ritzl A, Fink GR, Zilles K, Freund HJ, Rizzolatti G (2004) Neural circuits underlying imitation of hand actions: an event related fMRI study. Neuron 42: 323–34.

Colapietro V., (1988), "Human Agency: The Habits of Our Being." Southern Journal of Philosophy, XXVI, 2, pp. 153-68.

Colapietro V., (1992), "Purpose, Power, and Agency." The Monist, 75, 4 (October) pp. 423-44.

Colapietro V., (2003), "Signs and their vicissitudes: Meanings in excess of consciousness and functionality." Logica, Dialogica, Ideologica, a cure di Susan Petrilli e Patrizia Calefato (Milano: Mimesis), pp. 221-36.

Colapietro V., (2004a), "C. S. Peirce's Reclamation of Teleology." Nature in American Philosophy, ed. Jean De Groot (Washington, D.C.: Catholic

University Press of America), pp. 88-108.

Colapietro V., (2004b), "Portrait of a Historicist: An Alternative Reading of Peircean Semiotic." Semiotiche, 2/04 [maggio 2004], pp. 49-68.

Colapietro V., (2006), "Engaged Pluralism: Between Alterity and Sociality." The Pragmatic Century: Conversations with Richard J. Bernstein (Albany, NY: SUNY Press), pp. 39-68.

Colapietro V., (2009), "Habit, Competence, and Purpose." Forthcoming in The Transactions of the Charles S. Peirce Society. Calder AJ, Keane J, Manes F, Antoun N, Young AW (2000) Impaired recognition and experience of disgust following brain injury. Nature Neurosci 3: 1077–1078.

Carey DP, Perrett DI, Oram MW (1997) Recognizing, understanding and reproducing actions. In: Jeannerod M, Grafman J (eds) Handbook of neuropsychology. Vol. 11: Action and cognition. Elsevier, Amsterdam.

Carr L, Iacoboni M, Dubeau MC, Mazziotta JC, Lenzi GL (2003) Neural mechanisms of empathy in humans: a relay from neural systems for imitation to limbic areas. Proc Natl Acad Sci USA 100: 5497–5502.

Changeux JP, Ricoeur P (1998) La nature et la règle. Odile Jacob, Paris.

Cochin S, Barthelemy C, Roux S, Martineau J (1999) Observation and execution of movement: similarities demonstrated by quantified electroencephalograpy. Eur J Neurosci 11: 1839– 1842.

Chomsky Noam, (2017) Requiem for the American Dream

Chomsky Noam, (2016) Who Rules the World?

Chomsky Noam, (2010) How the World Works

Churchland, P.S. (1986), Neurophilosophy (Cambridge, MA: The MIT Press).

Churchland, P.S. & Ramachandran, V.S. (1993), 'Filling in: Why Dennett is wrong', in Dennett and His Critics: Demystifying Mind, ed. B. Dahlbom (Oxford: Blackwell Scientific Press).

Churchland, P.S., Ramachandran, V.S. & Sejnowski, T.J. (1994), 'A critique of pure vision', in Large- scale Neuronal Theories of the Brain, ed. C. Koch & J.L. Davis (Cambridge, MA: The MIT Press).

Crick, F. (1994), The Astonishing Hypothesis: The Scientific Search for the Soul (New York: Simon and Schuster).

Crick, F. (1996), 'Visual perception: rivalry and consciousness', Nature, 379.

Crick, F. & Koch, C. (1992), 'The problem of consciousness', Scientific American, 267.

Craig AD (2002) How do you feel? Interoception: the sense of the physiological condition of the body. Nature Rev Neurosci 3: 655–666.

Damasio, A (2003a) Looking for Spinoza. Harcourt Inc. Damasio A (2003b) Feeling of emotion and the self. Ann NY Acad Sci 1001: 253–261.

d'Aquili, Eugene. "Senses of Reality in Science and Religion." Zygon 17, no 4 (1982)

d'Aquili, Eugene. "The Biopsychological Determinants of Religious Ritual Behavior." Zygon 10, no. 1 (1975)

d'Aquili, Eugene. "The Myth-Ritual Complex: A Biogenetic Structural Analysis." Zygon 18, no. 3 (1983)

d'Aquili, Eugene, and Andrew Newberg. The Mystical Mind: Probing the Biology of Religious Experience. Minneapolis: Fortress Press, 1999.

Daly DD. 1958. Ictal affect. Am J Psychiatry.

Damasio, A. (1994) Descartes' Error: Emotion, Reason and the Human Brain. New York, Putnams.

Damasio, A. (1999) The Feeling of What Happens: Body, Emotion and the Making of Consciousness. London, Heinemann.

Darwin, C. (1859) On the Origin of Species by Means of Natural Selection. London, Murray.

Darwin, C. (1871) The Descent of Man and Selection in Relation to Sex. London, John Murray.

Darwin, C. (1872) The Expression of the Emotions in Man and Animals. London, John Murray; also published

1965, Chicago, University of Chicago Press.

Dawkins, M.S. (1987) Minding and mattering. In C. Blakemore and S. Greenfield (eds) Mindwaves. Oxford, Blackwell, 151-60.

Dawkins, R. (1976) The Selfish Gene. Oxford, Oxford University Press; a new edition, with additional material, was published in 1989.

Dawkins, R. (1986) The Blind Watchmaker. London, Longman.

Di Pellegrino G, Fadiga L, Fogassi L, Gallese V, Rizzolatti G (1992) Understanding motor events: A neurophysiological study. Exp Brain Res 91: 176–80.

Deikman, A.J. (2000) A functional approach to mysticism. Journal of Consciousness Studies 7(11-12), 75-91.

Delmonte, M.M. (1987) Personality and meditation. In M. West (ed.) The

Psychology of Meditation. Oxford, Clarendon Press, 118-32.

Dennett, D.C. (1987) The Intentional Stance. Cambridge, MA, MIT Press.

Dennett, D.C. (1988) Quining qualia. In A.J. Marcel and E. Bisiach (eds) Consciousness in Contemporary Science. Oxford, Oxford University Press, 42-77.

Dennett, D.C. (1991) Consciousness Explained. Boston, MA, and London, Little, Brown and Co.

Dennett, D.C. (1995a) Darwin's Dangerous Idea. London, Penguin.

Dennett, D.C. (1995b) The unimagined preposterousness of zombies. Journal of Consciousness Studies 2(4), 322-6.

Dennett, D.C. (1995c) Cog: steps towards consciousness in robots. In T. Metzinger (ed.) Conscious Experience. Thorverton, Devon, Imprint Academic, 471-87.

Dennett, D.C. (1995d) The path not taken. Behavioral and Brain Sciences 18, 252-3; commentary on N. Block, On a confusion about a function of consciousness. Behavioral and Brain Sciences 18, 227.

Dennett, D.C. (1996a) Facing backwards on the problem of consciousness. Journal of Consciousness Studies 3(1), 4-6.

Dennett, D.C. (1996b) Kinds of Minds: Towards an Understanding of Consciousness. London, Weidenfeld & Nicolson.

Dennett, D.C. (1997) An exchange with Daniel Dennett. In J. Searle (ed.) The Mystery of Consciousness. New York, New York Review of Books, 115-19.

Dennett, D.C. (1998) The myth of double transduction. In S.R. Hameroff, A.W. Kaszniak and A. C. Scott (eds) Toward a Science of Consciousness: The Second Tucson Discussions and

Debates. Cambridge, MA, MIT Press, 97-107.

Dennett, D.C. (1998b) Brainchildren: Essays on Designing Minds. Cambridge, MA, MIT Press.

Dennett, D.C. (2001) The fantasy of first person science. Debate with D. Chalmers, Northwestern University, Evanston, IL, February 2001.

Dennett, D.C. (2003) Freedom Evolves. New York, Penguin.

Dennett, D.C. and Kinsbourne, M. (1992) Time and the observer: the where and when of consciousness in the brain. Behavioral and Brain Sciences 15, 183-247, including commentaries and authors' responses.

Dewey J., (1911 [1977]), "Epistemological Realism: The Alleged Ubiquity of the Knowledge Relation." Journal of Philosophy, VIII, 20 (September 28, 1911).

Dewhurst, Kenneth, and A. W. Beard. "Sudden Religious Conversions in Temporal Lobe Epilepsy." British Journal of Psychiatry 117 (1970)

Dewhurst K, Beard AW. Sudden religious conversions in temporal lobe epilepsy. 1970 Epilepsy Behav 2003

Devinsky O, Lai G. Spirituality and religion in epilepsy. Epilepsy Behav 2008.

Devinsky, O., Morrell, MJ, Vogt, BA. (1995) 'Contribution of anterior cingulate cortex to behavior', Brain, 118.

Douglas Stone A., Chapter 24, The Indian Comet, in the book Einstein and the Quantum, Princeton University Press, Princeton, New Jersey, 2013.

E. Horvitz, "One Hundred Year Study on Artificial Intelligence: Reflections and Framing," ed: Stanford University, 2014.

Einstein A. (1925). "Quantentheorie des einatomigen idealen Gases". Sitzungsberichte der Preussischen Akademie der Wissenschaften.

Eckhart Meister, Selected Writings

Egidi R., ed. (1999), "Von Wright and 'Dante's Dream': Stages in a Philosophical Pilgrim's Progress", in In Search of a New Humanism: the Philosophy of G.H. von Wright, ed. by R. Egidi, Kluwer, Dordrecht.

Fadiga L, Fogassi L, Pavesi G, Rizzolatti G (1995) Motor facilitation during action observation: a magnetic stimulation study. J Neurophysiol 73: 2608–2611.

Fogassi L, Gallese V, Fadiga L, Rizzolatti G (1998) Neurons responding to the sight of goal directed hand/arm actions in the parietal area PF (7b) of the macaque monkey. Soc Neurosci Abs 24:257.5.

Frith U, Frith CD (2003) Development and neurophysiology of mentalizing. Philos Trans R Soc Lond B Biol Sci 358: 459.

Farah, M.J. (1989), 'The neural basis of mental imagery', Trends in Neurosciences, 10.

Finlay BL, Darlington RB (1995) Linked regularities in the development and evolution of mammalian brains. Science 268.

Freud, S. "The Interpretation of Dreams", 1900

Freud, S. "Selected papers on hysteria and other psychoneuroses" Journal of Nervous and Mental Disease 1909.

Freud, S. "The Origin and Development of Psychoanalysis", 1910

Freud, S. "Psychopathology of everyday life", 1914

Freud, S. "Beyond the Pleasure Principle", 1920

Frith, C.D. & Dolan, R.J. (1997), 'Abnormal beliefs: Delusions and memory', Paper presented at the May, 1997, Harvard Conference on Memory and Belief.

Gay, Volney, ed. Neuroscience and Religion. Plymouth, UK: Lexington Books, 2009.

Gazzaniga, M. S. (1985). The social brain. New York: Basic Books.

Gazzaniga, M.S. (1993), 'Brain mechanisms and conscious experience', Ciba Foundation Symposium, 174.

Geschwind N. "Behavioural changes in temporal lobe epilepsy". Psychol Med. 1979.

Gellhorn, E., Kiely, W.F. "Mystical states of consciousness: neurophysiological and clinical aspects." J Nerv Ment Dis. 1972;154:399-405.

Gilbert SL, Dobyns WB, Lahn BT (2005) Genetic links between brain development and brain evolution. Nat Rev Genet 6.

Gray JA. The Psychology of Fear and Stress. 2nd ed. New York, NY: Cambridge University Press; 1988.

Gloor, P. (1992), 'Amygdala and temporal lobe epilepsy', in The Amygdala: Neurobiological Aspects of Emotion, Memory and Mental Dysfunction, ed J.P. Aggleton (New York: Wiley-Liss).

Greenspan, S. I. and S. G. Shanker (2004). The first idea: How symbols, language, and intelligence evolved from our early primate ancestors to modern humans. Cambridge, MA: Da Capo Press.

Grady, D. (1993), 'The vision thing: Mainly in the brain', Discover, June.

Gallagher HL, Frith CD (2003) Functional imaging of 'theory of mind'. Trends Cogn Sci 7: 77.

Gallese V, Fogassi L, Fadiga L, Rizzolatti G (2002) Action representation and the inferior parietal lobule. In: Prinz W, Hommel B (eds) Attention & Performance XIX. Common mechanisms in perception and action. Oxford University Press, Oxford.

Gallese V, Keysers C, Rizzolatti G (2004) A unifying view of the basis of social cognition. Trends Cogn Sci 8: 396–403.

Gangitano M, Mottaghy FM, Pascual-Leone A (2001) Phase specific modulation of cortical motor output during movement observation. NeuroReport 12: 1489–1492.

Gangitano M, Mottaghy FM, Pascual-Leone A (2004) Modulation of premotor mirror neuron activity during observation of unpredictable grasping movements. Eur J Neurosci 20: 2193– 2202.

Goldman AI, Sripada CS (2004) Simulationist models of face-based emotion recognition. Cognition 94: 193–213.

Grèzes J, Costes N, Decety J (1998) Top-down effect of strategy on the perception of human biological motion: a PET investigation. Cogn Neuropsychol 15: 553–582.

Grèzes J, Armony JL, Rowe J, Passingham RE (2003) Activations related to "mirror" and "canonical" neurones in the human brain: an fMRI study. Neuroimage 18: 928–937.

Gross CG, Rocha-Miranda CE, Bender DB (1972) Visual properties of neurons in the inferotemporal cortex of the macaque. J Neurophysiol 35: 96–111.

Hari R, Forss N, Avikainen S, Kirveskari S, Salenius S, Rizzolatti G

(1998) Activation of human primary motor cortex during action observation: a neuromagnetic study. Proc. Natl Acad Sci USA 95: 15061–15065.

Hardy, G. H. (1940). Ramanujan. Cambridge: Cambridge University Press.

Hall, Daniel, Keith Meador, and Harold Koenig. "Measuring Religiousness in Health Research: Review and Critique." Journal of Religion and Health 47, no. 2 (2008)

Harris, Sam, Jonas Kaplan, Ashley Curiel, Susan Bookheimer, Marco Iacoboni, and Mark Cohen. "The Neural Correlates of Religious and Nonreligious Belief." PLoS One 4, no. 10 (October 1, 2009)

Halgren, E. (1992), 'Emotional neurophysiology of the amygdala within the context of human cognition', in The Amygdala:

Neurobiological Aspects of Emotion, Memory and Mental Dysfunction, ed J.P. Aggleton (New York: Wiley-Liss).

Halligan PW, Fink GR, Marshal JC, Vallar G. 2003. Spatial cognition: evidence from visual neglect. Trends Cogn Sci.

Handbook of Emotions, Edited by Michael Lewis, Jeannette M. Haviland-Jones, and Lisa Feldman Barrett, The Guilford Press; 3rd edition (2010).

Haggard, P., Clark, S. and Kalogeras,]. (2002) Voluntary action and conscious awareness, Nature Neuroscience 5, 382-5. Haggard, P., Newman, C. and Magno, E. (1999) On the perceived time of voluntary actions. British Journal of Psychology 90, 291-303.

Hameroff, S.R. and Penrose, R. (1996) Conscious events as orchestrated space-time selections. Journal of Consciousness Studies 3(1), 36-53; also reprinted in J. Shear (ed.) (1997)

Explaining Consciousness-The Hard Problem. Cambridge, MA, MIT Press, 177-95.

Hardcastle, V.G. (2000) How to understand theN in NCC. InT. Metzinger (ed.) Neural Correlates of Consciousness. Cambridge, MA, MIT Press, 259-64.

Harding, D.E. (1961) On Having no Head: Zen and the Re-Discovery of the Obvious. London, Buddhist Society.

Hardy, A. (1979) The Spiritual Nature of Man: A Study of Contemporary Religious Experience. Oxford, Clarendon Press.

Hamad, S. (1990) The symbol grounding problem. Physica D 42, 335-46.

Hamad, S. (2001) No easy way out. The Sciences 41(2), 36-42.

Harre, R. and Gillett, G. (1994) The Discursive Mind. Thousand Oaks, CA, Sage.

Haugeland, J. (ed.) (1997) Mind Design II: Philosophy, Psychology, Artificial Intelligence. Cambridge, MA, MIT Press.

Hauser, M.D. (2000) Wild Minds: What Animals Really Think. New York, Henry Holt and Co.; London, Penguin.

Hearne, K. (1990) The Dream Machine. Northants, Aquarian.

Hebb, D.O. (1949) The Organization of Behavior. New York, Wiley.

Helmholtz, H.L.F. von (1856-67) Treatise on Physiological Optics.

Hess, EH (1975) "The role of pupil size in communication," Scientific American, 233(5), 110–12.

Heyes, C.M. (1998) Theory of mind in nonhuman primates. Behavioral and

Brain Sciences 21, 101-48; with commentaries.

Heyes, C.M. and Galef, B.G. (eds) (1996) Social Learning in Animals: The Roots of Culture. San Diego, CA, Academic Press.

Hilgard, E.R. (1986) Divided Consciousness: Multiple Controls in Human Thought and Action. New York, Wiley.

Hitler, Adolf. Mein Kampf, 1925

Hodgson, R. (1891) A case of double consciousness. Proceedings of the Society for Psychical Research 7, 221-58.

Hofstadter, D.R. and Dennett, D.C. (eds) (1981) The Mind's I: Fantasies and Reflections on Self and Soul. London, Penguin.

Holland, J. (ed.) (2001) Ecstasy: The Complete Guide: A Comprehensive Look at the Risks and Benefits of

MDMA. Rochester, VT, Park Street Press.

Holmes, D.S. (1987) The influence of meditation versus rest on physiological arousal. In M. West (ed.) The Psychology of Meditation. Oxford, Clarendon Press, 81-103.

Holmstrom, David. 1992, Christian Science Monitor

Holt, J. (1999) Blindsight in debates about qualia. Journal of Consciousness Studies 6(5), 54-71.

Horgan, J. (1994), 'Can science explain consciousness?', Scientific American, 271.

Holloway RL (1996) Evolution of the human brain. In: Lock A, Peters CR (eds) Handbook of human symbolic evolution. Oxford University Press, Oxford

Iacoboni M, Woods RP, Brass M, Bekkering H, Mazziotta JC, Rizzolatti

G (1999) Cortical mechanisms of human imitation. Science 286: 2526–2528.

Iacoboni M, Koski LM, Brass M, Bekkering H, Woods RP, Dubeau MC, Mazziotta JC, Rizzolatti G (2001) Reafferent copies of imitated actions in the right superior temporal cortex. Proc Natl Acad Sci USA 98: 13995–13999.

Jeannerod M (1988) The neural and behavioural organization of goal-directed movements. Clarendon Press, Oxford.

Johnson-Frey SH, Maloof FR, Newman-Norlund R, Farrer C, Inati S, Grafton ST (2003) Actions or hand-objects interactions? Human inferior frontal cortex and action observation. Neuron 39: 1053–1058.

Jackson, F. (1982) Epiphenomenal qualia. Philosophical Quarterly 32, 127-36.

James, W. (1890) The Principles of Psychology (2 volumes). London, Macmillan.

James, W. (1902) The Varieties of Religious Experience: A Study in Human Nature. New York and London, Longmans, Green and Co.

Jansen, K. (2001) Ketamine: Dreams and Realities. Sarasota, FL, Multidisciplinary Association for Psychedelic Studies.

Jay, M. (ed.) (1999) Artificial Paradises: A Drugs Reader. London, Penguin.

Jaynes, J. (1976) The Origin of Consciousness in the Breakdown of the Bicameral Mind. New York, Houghton Mifflin.

Johnson, M.K. and Raye, C.L. (1981) Reality monitoring. Psychological Review 88, 67-85.

Kadim I, Mahgoub O, Baqir S et al. (2015) Cultured meat from muscle stem cells: a review of challenges and prospects. J Integr Agr 14: 222–233

Koski L, Iacoboni M, Dubeau MC, Woods RP, Mazziotta JC (2003) Modulation of cortical activity during different imitative behaviors. J Neurophysiol 89: 460–471.

Krolak-Salmon P, Henaff MA, Isnard J, Tallon-Baudry C, Guenot M, Vighetto A, Bertrand O, Mauguiere F (2003) An attention modulated response to disgust in human ventral anterior insula. Ann Neurol 53: 446–453.

Kandel, E. R. In Search of Memory: The Emergence of a New Science of Mind, W. W. Norton & Company (2007).

Kandel E. R. Schwartz JH, Jessel TM. Principles of neural sciences. New York; McGraw Hill, 2000.

Kanizsa, G. (1979), Organization In Vision (New York: Praeger).

Kaloupek DG, Scott JR, Khatami V. Assessment of coping strategies associated with syncope in blood donors. J Psychosom Res. 1985;29:207-214.

Kanwisher, N. (2001) Neural events and perceptual awareness. Cognition 79, 89-113; also reprinted inS. Dehaene (ed.) The Cognitive Neuroscience of Consciousness. Cambridge, MA, MIT Press, 89-113.

Kapleau, Roshi P. (1980) The Three Pillars of Zen: Teaching, Practice, and Enlightenment (revised edn). New York, Doubleday.

Karn, K. and Hayhoe, M. (2000) Memory representations guide targeting eye movements in a natural task. Visual Cognition 7, 673-703.

Kasamatsu, A. and Hirai, T. (1966) An electroencephalographic study on the Zen meditation (zazen). Folia

Psychiatrica et Neurologica Japonica 20, 315-36.

Kaiserman-Abramof, I. R., Graybiel, A. M., & Nauta, W. J. (1980). The thalamic projection to cortical area 17 in a congenitally anophthalmic mouse strain. Neuroscience, 5, 41–52.

Kanold, P. O., Kara, P., Reid, R. C., & Shatz, C. J. (2003). Role of subplate neurons in functional maturation of visual cortical columns. Science, 301, 521–525.

Kennedy, H., & Dehay, C. (1988). Functional implications of the anatomical organization of the callosal projections of visual areas V1 and V2 in the macaque monkey. Behav. Brain Res., 29, 225–236.

Kentridge, R.W. and Heywood, C.A. (1999) The status of blindsight. Journal of Consciousness Studies 6(5), 3-11.

Kihlstrom, J.F. (1996) Perception without awareness of what is perceived, learning without awareness of what is learned. In M. Velmans (ed.) The Science of Consciousness. London, Routledge, 23-46.

Kollerstrom, N. (1999) The path of Halley's comet, and Newton's late apprehension of the law of gravity. Annals of Science 56, 331-56.

Kosslyn, S.M. (1980) Image and Mind. Cambridge, MA, Harvard University Press.

Kosslyn, S.M. (1988) Aspects of a cognitive neuroscience of mental imagery. Science 240, 1621-6.

Kinsbourne, M. (1995), 'The intralaminar thalamic nucleii', Consciousness and Cognition, 4.

Kjaer, Troels, Camilla Bertelsen, Paola Piccini, David Brooks, Jorgen Alving, and Hans Lou. "Increased Dopamine Tone during Meditation- Induced Change of Consciousness." Cognitive Brain Research 13, no. 2 (April 2002)

Kölmel HW. 1985. Complex visual hallucinations in the hemianopic field. J Neurol Neurosurg Psychiatry.

Koenig, Harold. "Research on Religion, Spirituality, and Mental Health: A Review." Canadian Journal of Psychiatry 54, no. 5 (May 2009)

Koenig, Harold, ed. Handbook of Religion and Mental Health. San Diego, CA: Academic Press, 1998

Kraepelin E. Psychiatry: A Textbook for Students and Physicians. New York, NY: Science History Publications; 1990.

Lauglin, Charles, John McManus, and Eugene d'Aquili. Brain, Symbol, and Experience. 2nd ed. New York: Columbia University Press, 1992

Lakoff, G. and M. Johnson (1999). Philosophy in the flesh. Basic Books: New York.

LeDoux, J. E. (1996). The emotional brain. New York: Simon & Schuster.

LeDoux, J.E. (1992), 'Emotion and the amygdala', in The Amygdala: Neurobiological Aspects of Emo- tion, Memory and Mental Dysfunction, ed J.P. Aggleton (New York: Wiley-Liss).

Levin, D.T. and Simons, D.J. (1997) Failure to detect changes to attended objects in motion pictures. Psychonomic Bulletin and Review 4, 501-6.

Levine,J. (1983) Materialism and qualia: the explanatory gap. Pacific Philosophical Quarterly 64, 354-61.

Levine,J. (2001) Purple Haze: The Puzzle of Consciousness. New York, Oxford University Press. Levine, S. (1979) A Gradual Awakening. New York, Doubleday.

Levinson, B.W. (1965) States of awareness during general anaesthesia.

British Journal of Anaesthesia 37, 544-6.

Lewicki, P., Czyzewska, M. and Hoffman, H. (1987) Unconscious acquisition of complex procedural knowledge. Journal of Experimental Psychology: Learning, Memory and Cognition 13, 523-30.

Lewicki, P., Hill, T. and Bizot, E. (1988) Acquisition of procedural knowledge about a pattern of stimuli that cannot be articulated. Cognitive Psychology 20, 24-37.

Lewicki, P., Hill, T. and Czyzewska, M. (1992) Nonconscious acquisition of information. American Psychologist 47, 796-801.

Manthey S, Schubotz RI, von Cramon DY (2003). Premotor cortex in observing erroneous action: an fMRI study. Brain Res Cogn Brain Res 15: 296–307.

Mesulam MM, Mufson EJ (1982) Insula of the old world monkey. III: Efferent cortical output and comments on function. J Comp Neurol 212: 38–52.

Naskar, Abhijit. "Homo: A Brief History of Consciousness", 2015

Naskar, Abhijit. "What is Mind?", 2016

Naskar, Abhijit. "Love, God & Neurons: Memoir of A Scientist who found himself by getting lost", 2016

Naskar, Abhijit. "Principia Humanitas", 2017

Naskar, Abhijit. "We Are All Black: A Treatise on Racism", 2017

Naskar, Abhijit. "Either Civilized or Phobic: A Treatise on Homosexuality", 2017

Naskar, Abhijit. "I Am The Thread: My Mission", 2017

Naskar, Abhijit. "The Bengal Tigress: A Treatise on Gender Equality", 2017

Naskar, Abhijit. "Morality Absolute", 2017

Naskar, Abhijit. "Build Bridges not Walls: In the name of Americana", 2018

Naskar, Abhijit. "Fabric of Humanity", 2018

Naskar, Abhijit. "Lives To Serve Before I Sleep", 2019

Naskar, Abhijit. "Citizens of Peace: Beyond the Savagery of Sovereignty", 2019

Naskar, Abhijit. "The Constitution of The United Peoples of Earth", 2019

Naskar, Abhijit. "Neurons Giveth, Neurons Taketh Away | Abhijit Naskar | TEDxIIMRanchi", 2019 https://www.youtube.com/watch?v=BNX-Q0ySm80

Naskar, Abhijit. "Mission Reality", 2019

Naskar, Abhijit. "Operation Justice: To Make A Society That Needs No Law", 2019

Naskar, Abhijit. "Every Generation Needs Caretakers: The Gospel of Patriotism", 2020

Naskar, Abhijit. "Hurricane Humans: Give me accountability, I'll give you peace", 2020

Naskar, Abhijit. "Revolution Indomable", 2020

Naskar, Abhijit. "Servitude is Sanctitude", 2020

Naskar, Abhijit. "Good Scientist: When Science and Service Combine", 2020

Newberg, Andrew, and Jeremy Iversen. "The Neural Basis of the Complex Mental Task of Meditation: Neurotransmitter and Neurochemical Considerations." Medical Hypotheses 61, no. 2 (2003).

Newberg, Andrew. "How God Changes Your Brain: An Introduction to Jewish Neurotheology", CCAR Journal: The Reform Jewish Quarterly, Winter 2016.

Newberg, Andrew, and Stephanie Newberg. "A Neuropsychological Perspective on Spiritual Development." In Handbook of Spiritual Development in Childhood and Adolescence, edited by Eugene Roehlkepartain, Pamela King, Linda Wagener, and Peter Benson. London: Sage Publications, Inc., 2005

Newberg, Andrew. "The Neurotheology Link An Intersection Between Spirituality and Health", Alternative and Complimentary Therapies, Vol 21 No 1, February 2015.

Newberg, Andrew, Nancy Wintering, Dharma Khalsa, Hannah Roggenkamp, and Mark Waldman. "Meditation Effects on Cognitive Function and Cerebral Blood Flow in

Subjects with Memory Loss: A Preliminary Study." Journal of Alzheimer's Disease 20, no. 2 (2010)

Nash, M. (1995), 'Glimpses of the mind', Time.

Nesse RM. Proximate and evolutionary studies of anxiety, stress and depression: synergy at the interface. Neurosci Biobehav Rev. 1999;23:895-903.

Nicolelis, Miguel. (2011) "Beyond Boundaries: The New Neuroscience of Connecting Brains with Machines--- and How It Will Change Our Lives", Times Books

O'Hara, K. and Scutt, T. (1996) There is no hard problem of consciousness. Journal of Consciousness Studies 3(4), 290-302, reprinted in J. Shear (ed.) (1997) Explaining Consciousness. Cambridge, MA, MIT Press, 69-82.

O'Regan, J.K. (1992) Solving the "real" mysteries of visual perception: the world as an outside memory. Canadian Journal of Psychology 46, 461-88.

O'Regan, J.K. and Noe, A. (2001) A sensorimotor account of vision and visual consciousness. Behavioral and Brain Sciences 24(5), 883-917.

O'Regan, J.K., Rensink, R.A. and Clark,].]. (1999) Change-blindness as a result of "mudsplashes." Nature 398, 34.

Ornstein, R.E. (1977) The Psychology of Consciousness (2nd edn). New York, Harcourt.

Ornstein, R.E. (1986) The Psychology of Consciousness (3rd edn). New York, Pehguin.

Ornstein, R.E. (1992) The Evolution of Consciousness. New York, Touchstone.

Penfield W, Faulk ME (1955) The insula: further observations on its function. Brain 78: 445– 470.

Penrose, R. (1994), Shadows of the Mind (Oxford: Oxford University Press).

Penrose, R. (1989), The Emperor's New Mind: Concerning Computers, Minds and The Laws of Physics (Oxford: Oxford University Press).

Persinger, "'I would kill in God's name' role of sex, weekly church attendance, report of a religious experience and limbic lability" Perceptual and Motor Skills 1997.

Persinger "Experimental simulation of the God experience" Neurotheology 2003.

Persinger, M. A. (1993b). Personality changes following brain injury as a grief response to the loss of sense of self: Phenomenological themes as indices of local lability and neurocognitive restructuring as psycho- therapy. Psychological Reports, 72

Persinger, Corradini, Clement, Keaney, et al "Neurotheology and its convergence with neuroquantology" NeuroQuantology 2010.

Persinger, Koren and St-Pierre "The electromagnetic induction of mystical and altered states within the laboratory" Journal of Consciousness Exploration and Research 2010.

Persinger "Case report: A prototypical spontaneous 'sensed presence' of a sentient being and concomitant electroencephalographic activity in the clinical laboratory" Neurocase 2008.

Persinger and Saroka "Potential production of Hughlings Jackson's "parasitic consciousness" by physiologically-patterned weak transcerebral magnetic fields: QEEG and source localization" Epilepsy & Behavior 28 (2013).

Persinger. "The neuropsychiatry of paranormal experiences". J Neuropsychiatry Clin Neurosci 2001.

Persinger. "Neuropsychological bases of god beliefs", New York: Praeger, 1987

Persinger. "Temporal lobe epileptic signs and correlative behaviors displayed by normal populations", Journal of General Psychology, 1986

Perry BD, Pollard R. Homeostasis, stress, trauma, and adaptation. A neurodevelopmental view of childhood trauma. Child Adolesc Psychiatr Clin N Am. 1998;7:33.

Paré, D. & Llinás, R. (1995), 'Conscious and preconscious processes as seen from the standpoint of sleep-waking cycle neurophysiology', Neuropsychologia, 33.

P. S. de Laplace. Essai Philosophique sur les Probabilites [1814], in Academy des Sciences, Oeuvres Complotes de Laplace, Vol. 7, Gauthier-Villars, Paris (1886).

Perrett DI, Harries MH, Bevan R, Thomas S, Benson PJ, Mistlin AJ, Chitty AJ, Hietanen JK, Ortega JE (1989) Frameworks of analysis for the neural representation of animate objects and actions. J Exp Bio 146: 87–113.

Phillips ML, Young AW, Senior C, Brammer M, Andrew C, Calder AJ, Bullmore ET, Perrett DI, Rowland D, Williams SC, Gray JA, David AS (1997) A specific neural substrate for perceiving facial expressions of disgust. Nature 389: 495–498.

Phillips ML, Young AW, Scott SK, Calder AJ, Andrew C, Giampietro V, Williams SC, Bullmore ET, Brammer M, Gray JA (1998) Neural responses to facial and vocal expressions of fear and disgust. Proc R Soc Lond B Biol Sci 265: 1809–1817.

Puce A, Perrett D (2003) Electrophysiological and brain imaging of biological motion. Philosoph Trans Royal Soc Lond, Series B, 358: 435–445.

Ramachandran VS. Behavioral and magnetoencephalographic correlates of plasticity in the adult human brain. Proc Natl Acad Sci USA 1993; 90: 10413–20.

Ramachandran VS. Phantom limbs, neglect syndromes, repressed memories, and Freudian psychology. Int Rev Neurobiol 1994; 37: 291–333.

Ramachandran VS. Plasticity and functional recovery in neurology. Clin Med 2005; 5: 368–73.

Ramachandran VS, Hirstein W. The perception of phantom limbs. The D. O. Hebb lecture. Brain 1998; 121: 1603–30.

Ramachandran VS, Rogers-Ramachandran D, Cobb S. Touching the phantom limb. Nature 1995; 377: 489–90.

Ramachandran VS, Rogers-Ramachandran D. Phantom limbs and neural plasticity. Arch Neurol 2000; 57: 317–20.

Ramachandran VS, Rogers-Ramachandran D. It's all done with mirrors. Sci Am Mind 2007; 18: 16–9.

Ramachandran VS, Rogers-Ramachandran D. Sensations referred to a patient's phantom arm from another subjects intact arm: perceptual correlates of mirror neurons. Med Hypotheses 2008; 70: 1233–4.

Ramachandran VS, Rogers-Ramachandran D, Stewart M. Perceptual correlates of massive cortical reorganization. Science 1992; 258: 1159–60.

Rizzolatti G, Craighero L (2004) The mirror-neuron system. Annu Rev Neurosci 27: 169–192.

Rizzolatti G, Fogassi L, Gallese V (2001) Neurophysiological mechanisms underlying the understanding and imitation of action. Nature Rev Neurosci 2:661–670.

Rock I, Victor J. Vision and touch: an experimentally created conflict between the two senses. Science 1964; 143: 594–6.

Rose'n B, Lundborg G. Training with a mirror in rehabilitation of the hand. Scand J Plast Reconstr Surg Hand Surg 2005; 39: 104–8.

Royet JP, Plailly J, Delon-Martin C, Kareken DA, Segebarth C (2003) fMRI of emotional responses to odors: influence of hedonic valence and judgment, handedness, and gender. Neuroimage 20: 713–728.

Rozin R Haidt J and McCauley CR (2000) Disgust. In: Lewis M, Haviland-Jones JM (eds) Handbook of Emotion. 2nd Edition. Guilford Press, New York, pp 637–653.

Saxe R, Carey S, Kanwisher N (2004) Understanding other minds: linking developmental psychology and functional neuroimaging. Annu Rev Psychol 55: 87–124.

S. J. Russell and P. Norvig, Artificial intelligence: a modern approach (3rd edition): Prentice Hall, 2009.

Schienle A, Stark R, Walter B, Blecker C, Ott U, Kirsch P, Sammer G, Vaitl D (2002) The insula is not specifically involved in disgust processing: an fMRI study. Neuroreport 13: 2023–2026.

Showers MJC, Lauer EW (1961) Somatovisceral motor patterns in the insula. J Comp Neurol 117: 107–115.

Singer T, Seymour B, O'Doherty J, Kaube H, Dolan RJ, Frith CD (2004) Empathy for pain involves the affective but not the sensory components of pain. Science 303: 1157–1162.

Smith A (1759) The theory of moral sentiments (ed. 1976). Clarendon Press, Oxford.

S. N. Bose (1924). "Plancks Gesetz und Lichtquantenhypothese". Zeitschrift für Physik. 26 (1): 178–181.

Sprengelmeyer R, Rausch M, Eysel UT, Przuntek H (1998) Neural structures associated with recognition of facial expressions of basic emotions Proc R Soc Lond B Biol Sci 265: 1927–1931.

Strafella AP, Paus T (2000) Modulation of cortical excitability during action observation: a transcranial magnetic stimulation study. NeuroReport 11: 2289–2292.

Schilling, Vincent. 2017, indian country today

Stein, Stephen K. 2017, The Sea in World History: Exploration, Travel, and Trade

Simonsen R (2015) Eating for the future: veganism and the challenge of in vitro meat. In: Stapleton P, Byers A (Hg). Biopolitics and utopia. Palgrave Macmillan, New York (2015), S 167–190

Tanaka K (1996) Inferotemporal cortex and object vision. Ann Rev Neurosci. 19: 109–140.

Tesla N. "My Inventions", 1919

T. R. Society, "Machine learning: the power and promise of computers that learn by example," ed. The Royal Society, 2017.

Tomasello M, Call J (1997) Primate cognition. Oxford University Press, Oxford.

Tremblay C, Robert M, Pascual-Leone A, Lepore F, Nguyen DK, Carmant L, Bouthillier A, Theoret H (2004) Action observation and execution: intracranial recordings in a human subject. Neurology. 63: 937–938.

Umilta MA, Kohler E, Gallese V, Fogassi L, Fadiga L, Keysers C, Rizzolatti G (2001) "I know what you are doing": a neurophysiological study. Neuron 32: 91–101.

Von Wright G.H., (1963), Norm and Action. A Logical Inquiry, Routledge & Kegan Paul, London.

Von Wright G.H., (1976), "Determinism and the Study of Man", in Essays on Explanation and Understanding, ed. by J. Manninen and R. Tuomela, Reidel, Dordrecht.

Von Wright G.H., (1977), "What is Humanism?", The Lindlay Lecture, University of Arkansas, Lawrence, Kansas.

Von Wright G.H., (1979), "Humanism and the Humanities", in Philosophy and Grammar, ed. by S. Kanger and S. Öhman, Reidel, Dordrecht, pp. 1-16. Reprinted in von Wright (1993).

Von Wright G.H., (1980), Freedom and Determination, North-Holland Publishing Co., Amsterdam.

Von Wright G.H., (1985), Of Human Freedom, The Tanner Lectures on Human Values,

Vol. VI, ed. by S. M. McMurrin, University of Utah Press, Salt Lake City, pp. 107-70. Reprinted in von Wright (1998).

Von Wright G.H., (1993), The Tree of Knowledge and Other Essays, Brill, Leiden.

Von Wright G.H., (1997), "Progress: Fact and Fiction", in The Idea of Progress, ed. by A. Burgen et al., W. de Gruyter, Berlin, pp. 1-18.

Von Wright G.H., (1998), In the Shadow of Descartes: Essays in the Philosophy of Mind, Kluwer, Dordrecht.